me or us: a portrait

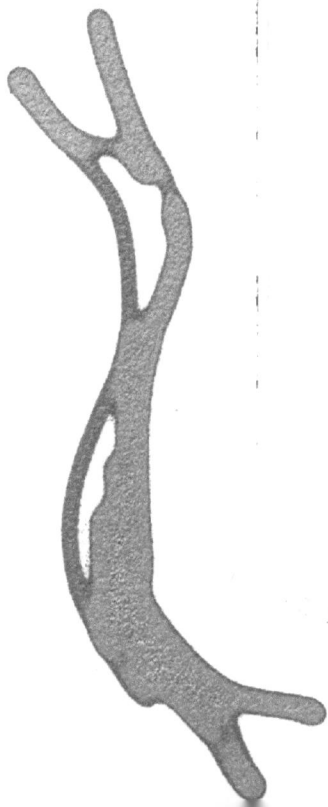

this book belongs to:

1

FERN

An insightful conversation between friends about the powers we possess

Justus

"GARRULOUS"

by S Ze LaBarge

A Conversational Introduction to:

Social Emotional Learning Concepts,

Critical Thinking for Independence,

Responsibility, Communication

Mindbody Health, Meditation

Logic and Systems ... and More!

{Scholar's Edition}

Likely Recommended For: Middle Grade and Up

2

These ideas try to cover the "common ground" foundations of thought, and thus allow for diversity in perspectives that go beyond them. Declarative statements in this book are backed by science and research, and likely contain nuance and range in their larger fields of study. The rest are posed as opinion and expression. This book is not intended to be used as professional advice and cannot be held liable.

Thank you to those who share a harmonious vision with me.

Thanks and dedication to:, in abbreviation: Lopez, LaBarge, Klein, Reas, Milburn, Hammonds, Mom, 23b, OC/LANC, Welch, KRA, Kentuckiana, and all my supporters and inspirers

Fern: "Hey Iustus. What's up ?"

Iustus: "Hey, Fern. School went smoothly. How are you?"

Fern: "Well, today, I felt stuck. Eventually, I realized I was seeking anyone else's solutions for that, not my own. So, I just sat in the grass all of lunch. That was nice."

4

Iustus: "I'm glad that worked. You know, Hans Selye said, 'Adapting the right attitude can convert a negative stress into a positive one.' Converting it even a little is nice. It requires being honest with yourself."

Fern: "Yeah, true. It's funny, when all is settled, nobody can live inside our heads to sort things out, to take action, but us. Self Agency is required."

Iustus: "It's funny, being in our own bodies and minds, because we drive our brain and body chemistry, but, it also drives us. When we use our attention span and concentration, we are depleting real chemicals in our brain. But, we can also train those processes to have better endurance, in most cases."

5

Fern: "So, we replenish our concentration by loosening focus for a while, otherwise. Yet, it's interesting to see the difference in our body's energy between what we like to do, and what we don't like to do, isn't it."

Iustus: "Yeah, because we get endorphins from certain activities. Those chemicals drive a lot of our interests, like learning, shopping, eating, and more, but... self awareness of even that can help, in the moment, or we can fall into unhealthy patterns. It helps if one can gamify, or make a game of, one's own life goals."

Fern: "Maybe that's like being in a flow state, like during a fun game, which has a fun challenge, but at our skill level. Life is still like that."

6

Justus: "Maybe sometimes we can 'befriend' our sense of pattern recognition as a part of us that is not entirely who we are. We are not our thoughts."

Fern: "Yeah. Because of pattern recognition, we have associations and relationships with nearly all aspects of life, including how we expect people to behave. Really, we cultivate the garden of our associations with aspects of life. Our adaptable sense of belief majorly influences our thinking, after all."

Justus: "I mean, that's the study of psychology. But, so much of psychology is circumstantial. A persuasive person, or a leader can really help set the tone for people's behavior. Also, people can experience change in circumstances, beliefs, and therefore seemingly change parts of their personality fairly quickly."   7

Fern: "You know, everything we and others think we know about the world makes up our unique paradigm, or overall perspective, of how the world works."

Justus: "It's funny, I mean, there is no exact replica of the moment we are living in, or the people in it, is there. There are few absolutes. Some people find zen in that, not futility."

Fern: "Well, I'd say overcompensating or overreacting because of feedback is one of humankind's most reliable skills. Haha."

Justus: "Okay, sure. Here's one: holding on to anger is like holding onto a hot coal to throw at your enemy. You are the one who gets burned."

Fern: "Yeah. Well, physiologically, sure, anger has an effect on the bearer. Hmm. It's like anger is just one possible reaction of many, not the best."

Iustus: "Yeah, well. I mean, there's tons of media out there where people study successful or happy people's beliefs, habits, and attitudes. That is, in whatever way they want to describe success."

Fern: "Yeah, like "grit," determination, appreciation, sure. When it comes to paradigms of how the world works, people must have paradigms and opinions about systems, too, even though systems have so many variable pieces."

Iustus: "Systems usually allow for measuring data because they have trackable events. Data analysis can, so to speak, paint a picture of reality by interpreting it in various ways through numbers and graphs, but this can also be done to make a misleading point. Graphs can still quickly show a bias, or also skewed proportions."

Iustus: "So, that's a good time to not think solely with your ego, so you can think about the implications of your own data and analysis instead."

Fern: "Yeah, you know, that's true. The ego, the part of the self that considers its place in society and implications in various contexts, has its uses. But for many, isolation is something that causes people to remain stuck without new insights in their life and relationships. But there are so many ways to find good peers and community in the modern world, in most cases.'"

Iustus: "Yeah, it doesn't have to be too hard. Social dynamics do vary, though."

Fern: "People talk about there being implied rules of conversation, which are definitely a matter of opinion and circumstance, don't you think?"

Iustus: Yes. I think what people do have are degrees of vulnerability, interest, curiosity, emotional availability, ideals, emotionality, relatability, and so on. There's more to it than that, but that's a good start."

Fern: "People like to be liked, listened to, and included. I mean, those are all very broad general statements. But when you begin to understand what drives people, you can get somewhere with that."

77

Iustus: "People do often speak from their pain points, like venting about anything unpleasant, or nearly wagging their tail like a dog with happiness."

Fern: "Haha. Hmm. I find it tactical to find some common goals with people."

Iustus: "Okay, but so are: infusing positive kindness, using humor, gauging one's audience, and, avoiding being self-righteous, since it's a vicious cycle of punishment."

12

Fern: "Don't forget: A willingness to be wrong sometimes."

Iustus: "Well, beyond being aware of those strategies, it is definitely not always our job to figure everyone out. There may be unspoken agreements in society and culture, but those "agreements" can be short-lived, flexible, trends, works in progress, contextual learned behaviors, so on."

Fern: "Well that's why civility, and the ongoing intention of true kindness goes so far. You know, Iustus, people may say you and I are "garrulous," but we sure built a good friendship around communication. We have our own understandings."

13

Iustus: "I agree. ... As for others, some people have more accurate intuition than others. Luckily I have even more methods for "listening" to myself. I make a *mind map* to note what's on my mind, so I can be assured I covered what I care about, and then let it go sometimes. I reevaluate freely."

SELF
- massage neck
- stretch
-

SATURDAY

SCHOOL
Research Clubs
okay

Hobby/Business
- make _____ later time

J's
Mind map

HOME
- ask to move chores to 3 days
- hammock?

yearbook *yes!*

friends

SOCIAL
- plan picnic?

14

Fern: "I bet that helps you keep from feeling overwhelmed."

Iustus: "Yes, but, I still have to prioritize the goals and tasks. The final list either fits on the calendar, and works out with my life, or not. I can always adapt it all."

Fern: "Yeah, for me, using predictable habits and planned activities is much easier than just using willpower to pull through everything and think of it on the spot. "

Iustus: "It's funny, it's also a skill to be good at being bad at things. That could mean you're okay with learning slower, taking criticism, watching others succeed, and, you adapt."

Fern: "Yeah. You evaluate, and you try again. Being caught up on self-worth ideas in this world can be distracting. If we keep getting data to work with, we can test our own theories and game plan, it doesn't matter what examples exist in the world, because we are bringing out the best in ourselves."

Iustus: "Like having a hypothesis, as part of the scientific method. Cool. But, yeah, there's more to being part of a team."

16. Scope of Project Task Delegation Deadlines

Fern: "When people see you taking responsibility, which may mean dealing with chaos and problems well, being fair, having a clear worthy vision and good motives, and getting good results,

they may want to give you more:

trials, chances, power, leadership, allowances, freedom, decision-making power, business, so on. It's a win-win situation."

Iustus: "Those people have incentive to trust you, because they want good results too. That's just one idea, which is nestled within others. But those are some foundations of business."

Fern: "But, not everything needs to be transactional in life."

Iustus: "I mean, there's plenty of ways people currently survive and thrive. They would be: gaining knowledge and wisdom about financial well-being, asset building, homesteading, crisis prevention, health, world ecosystems and agriculture, collaboration, systems, problem-solving, insight, and creativity-- among other things."

Fern: "I say, we could try to design opportunities for ourselves.

Could we garden? Fix bikes? Cook food? Use computers?

We won't let society, or even circumstance, sum up our worth for us."

Iustus: "Sometimes society and the world could use a healthy change, couldn't they. They need their value system addressed, evaluating both tradition and new changes."

Fern: "We ask, how will we be part of the change? Can we take breaks from it sometimes and then go back to it? What makes the people in charge listen? When is it okay to compromise? Is there a bigger picture to see, so to speak? I'm not saying it's easy."

Iustus: "Speaking of our contributions, it's time to do chores. You know, if you look at a giant messy gross sink like this, you might avoid it because it's intimidating."

Fern: "Really, we can come up with a strategy, or even a game, for lots of things like this. We can run experiments."

Iustus: "Okay, so then, doing dishes is a system, with measurable variables, such as time. Let's try doing the dishes for only 5 minutes. Then, see how far we got. ... Was it more or less than you thought, Fern?"

20

Fern: "It was easy with both of us.

You know, not everybody is great at thinking critically, or abstractly. But the more you try, the more you build up your brain powers to do it, even to visualize it, so on. That's how some people do math in their head."

Justus: "People should look into critical thinking, communication, modes of thinking, and creativity concepts. It's insightful, if they want to get better at it."

Fern: "You know what, In Cognitive Priming, the brain experiences a task or stimulus, and then it is prepped to perform the next function in a similar way as that first one. For an example... say silk 10 times fast! ...

Ok. Now, what does a cow drink? ... Yes, but, it's for the calf. Ha ha."

21

Iustus: "Okay I fell for it. Well, let's say we needed more ways to think about our dirty dishes problem. Convergent Thinking, or where ideas converge into one solution, is thinking sequentially about known elements of the problem, coming to one best solution. {Objective:The dishes need to be done. So: Wash them thoroughly.}

Whereas Divergent Thinking is thinking with parallels to the elements of the problem that diverge into multiple solutions. {Objectives: Remove smell and germs, complete as fast as possible, remove the dishes. So: Maybe the dishes can be sterilized with boiling water and stored under the sink.}

It's often good to think with imagination, intuition and rationale together, which is sometimes called Lateral Thinking ... {Blow up the dishes!}."

Fern: "Okay, I'm not sure there's an easily rationalized or justified situation for blowing up the dishes .... yet."

22

Fern: "I'll show you a bit more.

Logic deals with ideas of finding and testing truth.

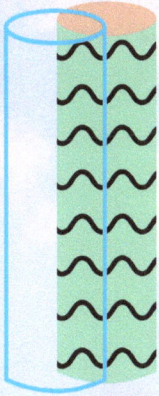

If you take a general statement like:

It's always better to do your homework.

Logic says that, if there's exists a case like this:

I didn't need any more points to get an A, and I had other

things to do, so it was not better to do the homework.

Then: It's NOT always better to do your homework.

23

Thus we have proved that

the previous general statement

is not true, by counterexample.

Yet one could say:

Most of the time, it's better to do your homework.

This allows your statement to be more inclusive of scenarios.

In real life, people would have to agree on the definition of

the words, their syntax, and applicable context in the

statements. Logic using numbers is therefore more accurate.

'Logic' can cause shortsightedness in decisions about systems in reality. It's easy to find lists of common biases and fallacies.

Also, in language, people often speak casually, taking verbal shortcuts, perhaps accessing their emotions, and they don't always include precise logical statements, for better or worse. Emoting is natural, and it's a form of thought. Logical shortcuts are called heuristics, which are 'good enough' for the purpose. It's present in what we've said today." 25

Justus: "Also, in discussion, allowing some room to grow for the other person is wise. You would gain teammates rather than enemies. Also, an engineer who forgets spelling may be deep in use of mathematical, visualizing, or perceptive abilities and so on."

Fern: "We all think differently, perceive a little differently. Some of us think more visually, wordlessly, intuitively, maybe audio-based, in verbal narrative, in emotion, in logical analysis, or more, or all of the above."

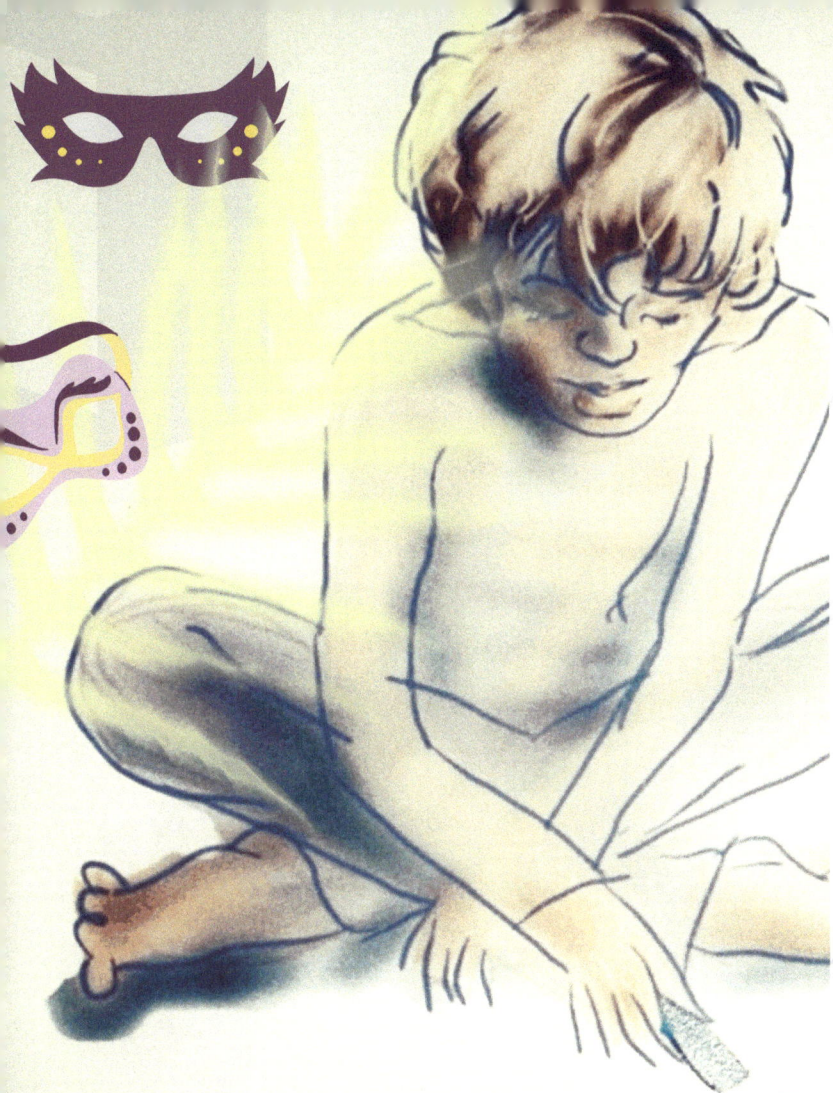

Iustus: "A form of Creativity I like is Free Association, which is speaking, drawing, playing, daydreaming, or doing whatever comes to mind.

It shows us expressions of parts of our personal value system. Me, I draw plants because I value how biology combines function and beauty. So cool."

Fern: "That is cool."

Iustus: "People say I draw plants to avoid social topics, which isn't true."

'Fern: "When it comes to your identity, you try to thrive as you, evaluate your influences, and develop and use your value system, because that's what counts. You will add your unique interpretation to aspects of life.

Like with dancing.

Most cultures on earth dance.

Good dancing has taken

so many shapes

and it will take so many more,

because it combines form, function,

aesthetics, expression, and other

value systems, like we do."

28

Iustus: "Yeah, you can't please everybody."

Justus: "Historically, you know, bugs have had to guess each other's approachability by using their senses and developed instinct from over many encounters. Humans also do this somewhat, and organize their ideas about what they experience. But, we can use logic and analyze information, which tells us that not every bug or human acts the way its looks say it should in the 'patterns' we thought we saw."

Fern: "It's funny, humans have to focus on finding common goals between differing groups to combat divisive political tactics. A lot more money changes hands in some businesses when people think they have enemies they can't negotiate with." 29

Iustus: "Ah. Well. It's a good thing I can cheer myself up. Like with Affirmations, which are beneficial thoughts we think and affirm within ourselves, like thoughts of our self worth, things to be grateful for, positive perspectives, so on. You want to hear more?

I like to affirm often that I'm on track for everything that I care about, that I can get on track easily, that I have plenty of time to make needed changes, that I can always get new data for new insights, and that in the end, I'll have done a great enough job. I did the best I could think of doing."

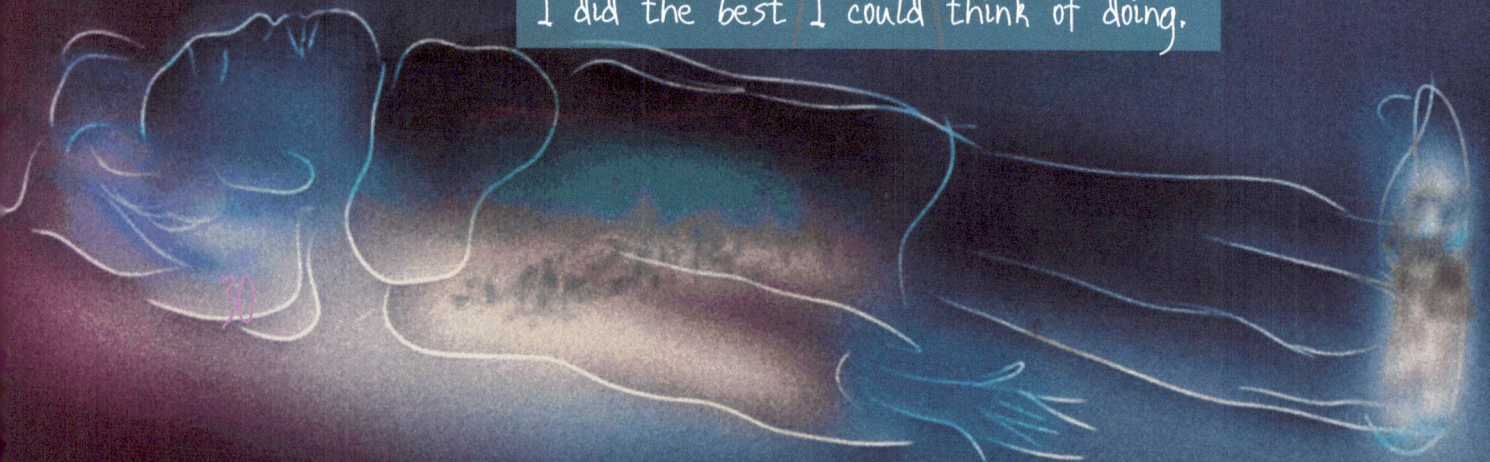

Fern: "Hmm. Very nice. Me, I like a fresh view, a fresh start, whenever I need it. No guilt, no self judgement. I can reset my expectations, to then set crafted patterns or plans in motion. Learned Helplessness is thinking we can't do anything about something. We can be Proactive, or, choosing to seek and take action.

You could say, you happen to things, or things just happen to you."

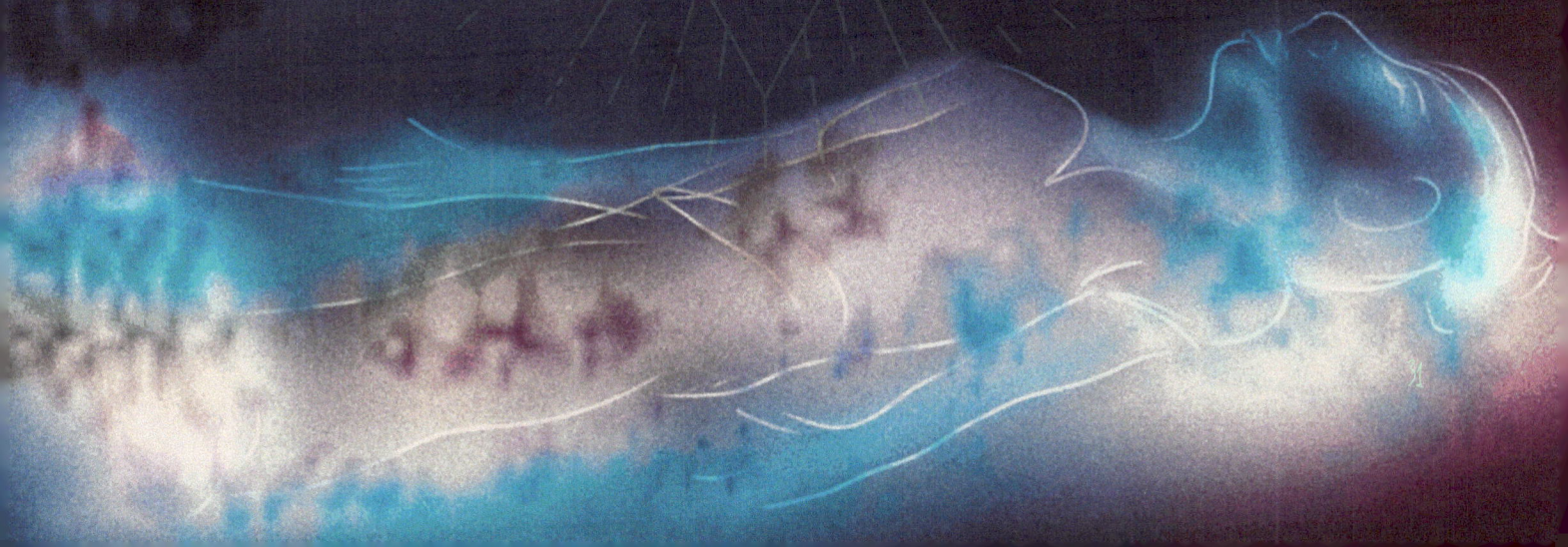

Iustus: "Well, for relaxing, there's also Progressive Muscle Relaxation. So, find any restful, physically balanced position. Breathe from your belly, not your chest, but listen to your bodies signals, too. Gently start from your head or toes, acknowledging or squeezing your muscles, then relaxing them. Keep imagining the tension of your muscles disappearing, across your body.

This is also a mind-body connection exercise, where you check in on and unite the 'perspectives' of parts and functions of your mind and body. An example of a 'disconnection:' You were so focused on a game, your leg became numb and also lost blood flow. But, you checked in."

32

Fern: "Yeah. That has similarities to a Bliss Meditation, where you take sensations that give you bliss or happiness, and you practice filling your whole mind and body with the thoughts and sensations.

You get better at these every time you do them.

There is also Loving Kindness Meditation, where you meditate on, or create a sensation of, goodwill toward all. I made up another scenario for this, where everyone alive is only 'two tied knots away from enlightenment,' and in my meditation the whole world becomes kind toward all with me as I do."

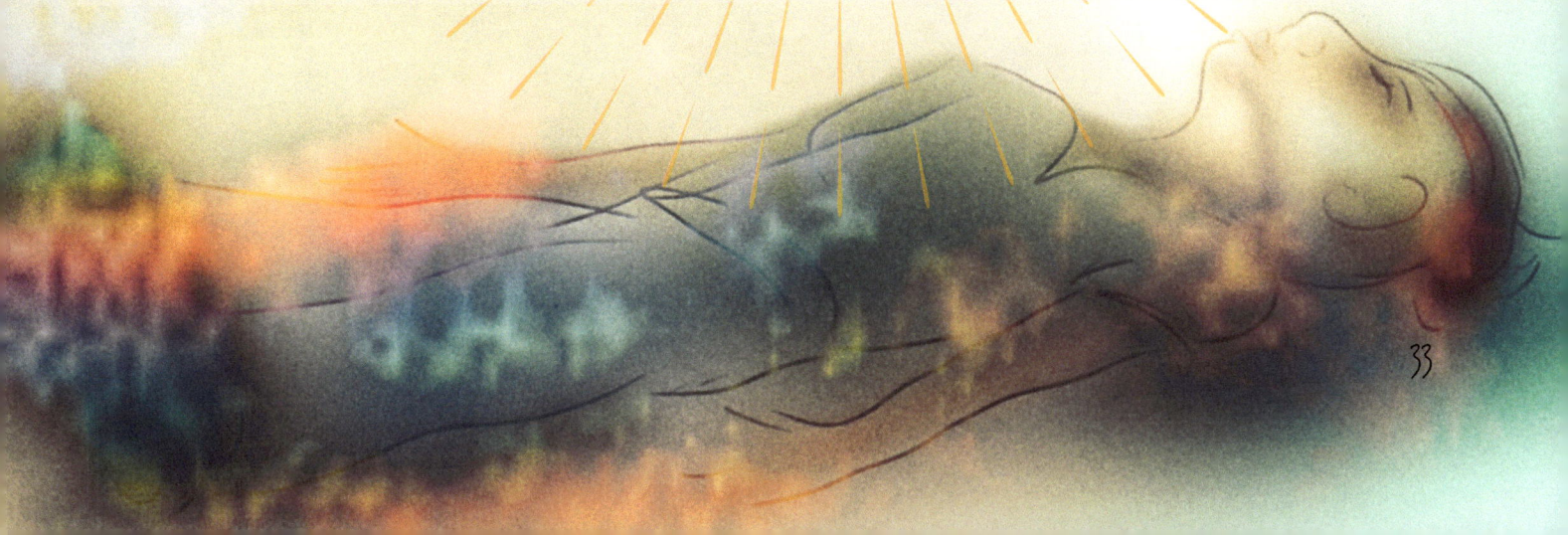

33

Iustus: "Very nice. It's also important to reduce stimulation and rest your nervous systems sometime. One can sort of let go with or without a story to go through.

But sometimes you might be out of balance, feeling at odds with everything. I'd hate for anyone to just give up when that happens.

There can be change!"

Fern: "I suppose we judge ourselves and others pretty hard sometimes, and feel powerless."

34

Iustus: "Yeah. Maybe you carry hard labels, heavy burdens,

grief, loneliness, --feel cruel, out of touch, numb,

afraid, desperate, undesirable.

--That your coping mechanisms resemble hoarding, binge eating,

obsessions, compulsions, addictions, or other undesirable extremes.

Maybe you're leaning on someone, you're overwhelmed by change,

you "fight / flight / freeze / faint / fawn", the stress responses.

You can be ok even when it's not so ok.

In hard times, try to gain a new 'torch in the dark.'

Don't stay on any downward spirals for very long, start on an upward

spiral. Those are just metaphors, but, perception counts."

35

Fern: "I find that if you keep seeking distraction, you will nearly always find it. Yet, it helps to have something to look forward to.

Painful mindstates have their place. If someone wants out, it's time to get back toward balance, hop on the upward spiral, no matter how slow the process."

Justus: "Ah. What do you suggest?"

36

Fern: "You find a little contentment, seek growth, adjust your values, affirm your strengths and resources, practice self-control sessions, build doable routines, use meditations, use affirmations, review good materials, do new research, forgive yourself,

and make appropriate memorials for the precious, if you wish.

Tune into curiosity and exploration,

let yourself renew and revive, carve a new path

and be someone else's torch in their darkness!

I'd want to be that torch for someone, or you."

Justus: "That's great to hear."

Iustus: "Well, myself I prefer to wrap up ideas in the light of their absurdity. In a certain light, every aspect of reality is goofy and can be given a spin, or, retold in a different light regarding motivations, outcome, and so on. But absurdity might loosen the grip that seemingly relevant drama has on us.

Tarry, ho there, friend, I hath forgotten mine round bumper and my plant-stained fabric-upon-stick.

Ah, what misfortune.

We suspend our normal perceptions and meaning-making. Ideas and values can be seen within various contexts, and measured from each frame of reference, or vantage point. Take deep ocean fish: in some way, are they "flying" above the sea floor, because they don't know birds exist, from their point of view?

In a certain light, morals, good and bad, right and wrong, they relate to the specific circumstance, and to each observer, so we say they are relative values. This does not skew objective (not a matter of opinion) reality, just subjective (a matter of opinion) judgements. Each viewpoint has its own merits, and data."

Fern: "Knights? Who wear metal coverings and metal poking sticks? For a symbol on fabric? Absurd. From the viewpoint of an outsider."

Justus: "Exactly. So when we are making meaning out of our lives, we must think critically for ourselves, because we will have to make a stand to try for what we value, no matter how 'odd,' but we can stay open-minded."

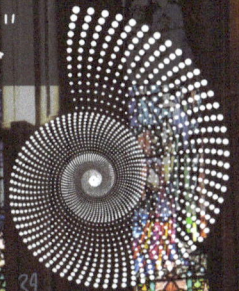

Fern: "Yes. As you know, after all that, some very important ideas remain:

Maybe humanity can work together

to grow to use its potential, fulfill its needs, and protect its earth and animals,

so it can participate in the larger realities of our solar system and beyond. Maybe

people can be more exploratory and open-minded about complexity in reality."

Iustus: "That's what makes for a cosmic perspective.

Good thinking today, my cosmic friend."

Some Additional Concepts for Research

Peer Pressure	ASMR
Sustainability in Ecosystems	Project Management
Sustainability in Systems	Parasympathic Activation
Befriending your "Shadow"	Sympathetic Dominance
Productivity Tools	Conditioning (Pyschology)
Meditation	Something/Nothing to Prove
Posture, Ergonomics	Endorphins, Dopamine,
Spin in Journalism	Serotonin, Oxytocin Influence
Accountability	Hormone Balance
Stigma and Tabboo	Nutrition Concepts
Dualities and Dichotomies	Systems

Self Fulfilling Prophecy

Gamification Concepts

Priming (Psychology)

Ableism, Meritocracy, Etc

Breathing for Intramuscular Oxygenation

Proprioception: Physical Balance

Cult-like Behaviors

Deconstruction in Language

Hypnosis, Self Hypnosis

Marginalization, Imperialism

Utilitarianism, Etc

Confirmation Bias, Etc

And of course, there are many other foundational and explorational topics out there.

The ability to "just be" is here presented to thee.

SBL

Yes, everything I've mentioned can indeed be deconstructed and reframed. 🌸

Glossary of Selected Terms

Lightly referencing Oxford Advanced Learner's Dictionary, Oxford English Dictionary

Association — a link between two ideas or entities. In psychology, a link made in the mind with a stimulus (any of the 5 senses) with another concept.

Centeredness — When referring to emotion: calm, sensible and emotionally in control. It is okay to be thrown off center by life events; it is nice to regain centeredness and clarity afterward.

Convergent — Coming closer together, especially in concepts or ideas. In math, lines can converge into a point by leading closer together, then meeting.

Cosmic Perspective — A general philosophical perspective that is based around the expanses, forces, structures, and various implications of a larger universe that Earth and its inhabitants must interface with, even someday. This tends to emphasize humankind's need to collaborate for heightened achievements, as opposed to having unending shallow goals and quarrels.

Critical Thinking — The objective analysis and evaluation of an issue in order to form a judgment. A skill set for reasonably successful judgment making and formation of wisdom.

45

Divergent — (of thought) (Divergent Thinking) Using a variety of premises, especially unfamiliar premises, as bases for inference, and avoiding common limiting assumptions in making deductions. Also, separating paths, especially regarding ideas. (Example in book: doing dishes)

Free Association — The mental process by which one word or image may spontaneously suggest another without any apparent connection. The reactive association which is not necessarily established in its purposefulness, depth, or longevity, by itself.

Futility — Pointlessness or uselessness. Subjective.

46

Learned Helplessness – An apathetic condition (and, psychological concept) in an animal or a human being resulting from exposure to unsolved problems or inescapable physical or emotional stress. Example: a baby elephant is tied to a chair and cannot leave, and in full-strength adulthood, it thinks that when it's tied to a chair, it still can't leave.

Paradigm – A philosophical or theoretical set of ideas, standards, and perspectives. Or: A typical example or pattern of something; a model. Example: A paradigm in 21st century education is the notion that people learn better in groups. Example: I had a paradigm shift when learning virtually by myself.

47

Parasympathetic Nervous System – The set of structures that make up the parasympathetic nervous system are responsible for, among other things, the body's rest and digestion response when the body is relaxed, resting, feeding, or otherwise parasympathetically stimulated.

Sympathetic Nervous System – The set of structures in the body's nervous system that, among other things, initiates rapid involuntary processes like increased heart rate that go along with excitement and stress.

Subjective / Objective — Whether something is relative in value (so, a matter of opinion), or precise in an exact statement of truth as understood in the defined terms (not a matter of opinion). Objective Example: The common pencil is 19 centimeters long in defined modern industrial standards. Subjective Example: The common pencil is too long. Used also in Physics, etc, differently.

Glossary Contents

49

www.ingramcontent.com/pod-product-compliance
Lightning Source LLC
Chambersburg PA
CBHW060856270326
41934CB00003B/168